Fields of Dreams

Wind-tossed meadow near Crested Butte, Colorado

FIELDS of DREAMS

Travels in the Wildflower Meadows of America

Text and Photographs by Tim Fitzharris
Foreword by Sue Hubbell

HarperSanFrancisco
A Division of HarperCollins*Publishers*

Acknowledgements begin on p. 72.

Produced by Terrapin Books, Santa Fe, New Mexico.

First Edition

Library of Congress Cataloging-in-Publication Data

Fitzharris, Tim, 1948-
    Fields of Dreams: travels in the wildflower meadows of America / text and photographs by Tim Fitzharris : foreword by Sue Hubbell.
        p. cm.
    Includes bibliographical references (p. 72).
    ISBN 0-06-251143-2 (pbk.)
    1. Wild flowers—United States. 2. Meadows—United States. 3. Meadow Ecology—United States. 4) Wildflowers—United States—Pictorial works. I. Title.
QK110.F54 1995
582. 13'0973—dc20   94-30222
                       CIP

ISBN 0-06-251143-2

95 96 97 98 99   TER   10 9 8 7 6 5 4 3 2 1

Printed in Hong Kong

California poppy meadow, Antelope Valley, California

For Don, Cora, Noah, and Erica

Other Books by Tim Fitzharris

The Adventure of Nature Photography
The Island
The Wild Prairie
Wildflowers of Canada (with Audrey Fraggalosch)
British Columbia Wild
Canada: A Natural History (with John Livingston)
Wild Birds of Canada
Forest: A National Audubon Society Book
The Audubon Society Guide to Nature Photography
Wild Wings: An Introduction to Birdwatching
Coastal Wildlife of British Columbia (with Bruce Obee)
The Sierra Club Guide to 35 mm Landscape Photography
The African Waterhole (with Audrey Fraggalosch)
Soaring with Ravens
Musings of Safari

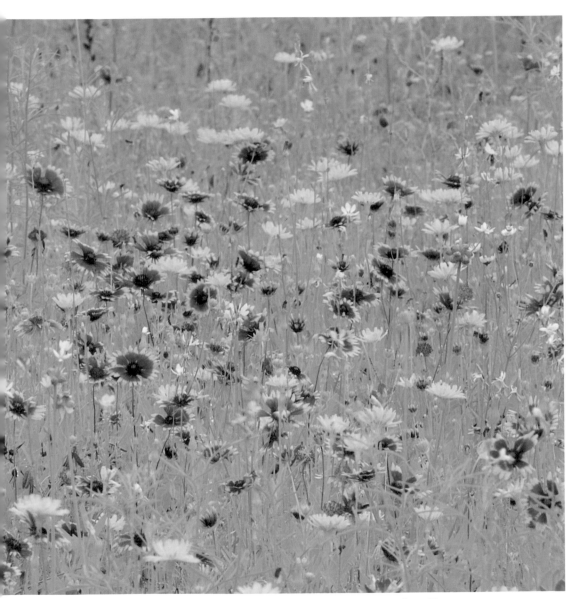

Indian blanket, coreopsis, and evening primrose meadow, Texas

Yellow pond lily and dragonfly

Wind-tossed daisies, Bonaventure Island, Quebec

Foreword

When I was a little girl growing up in the 1930's in southern Michigan, I knew the long winter was over when my father would ask me if I thought the trailing arbutus might be in bloom. Hadn't we best go pay it a visit and see? The first time I can clearly remember him asking me that question I was too young to be able to pronounce its common name, let alone its Latin binomial, *Epigaea repens*, with which he always accompanied its English name. But I already knew what he was talking about, remembered that it was special, pretty, and smelled good, so he must have been taking me to that place which had been his mother's family's farm from the time I could walk beside him.

Trailing arbutus, even then, was scarce throughout its native range in the eastern United States. Prized for its sweetness, the attractiveness of its white-pink flowers, and its promise of fair weather to come, it had been nearly eradicated by overzealous harvesting. My father told me that in earlier days the long, trailing, hairy stems with their evergreen leaves and fragrant flowers had been ripped up from the dry piney woods where the plant had grown and hawked on city streets in garlands. He was trained as a botanist, made his living as a landscape architect.

My father, B. LeRoy Gilbert, had, already in the 1920's when garden fashion dictated the planting of exotics, made a name for himself by using native plants in his designs. But trailing arbutus, he said, should never be dug. Too shy, too sensitive to disturbance, the plant would not grow after transplant.

That farm where the trailing arbutus grew was by then no longer owned by my grandmother's family, but I suspect my father had spent long hours walking it as a youngster, for he knew the land well. Perhaps he learned his love of wild things there. I never knew. By the time I had sense enough to wonder about his early life and how he became the man he was, he had been dead for years and I could no longer ask.

A portion of that farm was hard to get to and home to other rare and striking wildflowers—large-flowered trilliums which should not be picked lest the roots die and pink lady slippers, or moccasin flowers, which also transplanted poorly and, even then, nearly 60 years ago, had been overpicked. There were other commoner wildflowers that I first met in that hidden wild place: dog-toothed violets, with their nodding yellow heads that were not true violets at all but better named

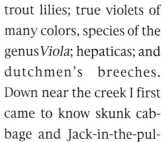

trout lilies; true violets of many colors, species of the genus *Viola*; hepaticas; and dutchmen's breeches. Down near the creek I first came to know skunk cabbage and Jack-in-the-pulpit. The old meadow, long untilled, would be full of daisies, Queen Anne's lace, and coreopsis when we came back later in the year with a picnic.

Picking the common ones, any of them, even the daisies, seemed inappro-

Indian blankets, Texas

Daisy and yellow hawkweed near Ithaca, New York

priate. My father, telling me the stories of their growth, reproduction, and rela-tionship to their surroundings, gave me the understanding that they were so at home that to take them away never entered my mind. To see them, we needed to go to where they grew.

Back at home I filled a little girl's need to gather pretty things by picking fistfuls of dandelions from the lawn and stuffing them into peanut butter jars. Today I don't even do that; I leave those golden blossoms, a rich source of nectar, for my honey bees.

I have not been back to that old Michigan farm in 50 years, would not know how to find it even if I wanted to. But I know other wildflower woods, bogs, and meadows. Each visit is built on the foundation of a gentle man's instruction in appropriateness and awe to a toddler for whom Latin was hard but beauty was not.

—Sue Hubbell

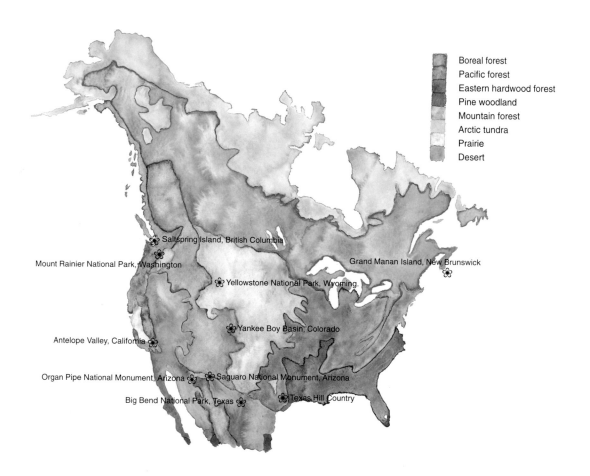

Boreal forest
Pacific forest
Eastern hardwood forest
Pine woodland
Mountain forest
Arctic tundra
Prairie
Desert

Saltspring Island, British Columbia

Mount Rainier National Park, Washington

Grand Manan Island, New Brunswick

Yellowstone National Park, Wyoming.

Yankee Boy Basin, Colorado

Antelope Valley, California

Organ Pipe National Monument, Arizona   Saguaro National Monument, Arizona

Big Bend National Park, Texas   Texas Hill Country

xvi

Cartography by Beverly Schrengohst

Introduction
Fields for Dreaming

Cows, butterflies and butterfly collectors, lovers, and botanists have vested interests in wildflower meadows. If you do not fall into one of these categories, you may think they hold nothing of value for you. But meadows are also for dreamers and that includes nearly everyone.

Some tips for dreaming in meadows which I found useful in preparing this book are as follows:

1) Lay down. Visually, this throws the flowers and grasses up against the sky making it possible to shift your view from the intimate to the infinite without moving anything but your ciliary muscles. Don't shift too fast or too often.

2) Eat first. If your stomach is content, your brain will be able to roam to great altitudes through multiple dimensions.

3) Apply insect repellent and, if necessary, take some antihistamines. With your face at flower level, this kind of protection is essential if you expect to be able to concentrate on nothing.

4) Clear days with a few cumulous clouds yield the best results. Without a standard shape, size, or position in the universe, clouds are inspirational models for your thoughts. The blue, of course, is a vacuum.

5) Choose meadows away from highways or factories. There are plenty of these in rural areas all over the continent. Among my favorites are those noted on the map. These are coincidentally some of the most beautiful meadows to be found anywhere.

Prickly Pear Cactus (*Opuntia Polycantha*) Flowers: bright yellow or orange, showy, large, 2 to 3 inches across; many sepals, petals, and stamens; 1 pistil of several united carpels Fruit: a soft, spiny, sweet, edible berry. Leaves: None, repre-

Desert Meadows
Bones of Hope and Memory

The sky is calm on most of the desert mornings of my recollection. It spreads above, not as the heavens on a summer night in the tropics, not as a wall of blue, but as a cloud that hovers about your head, a blanket of fine feeling imperceptibly draped about the shoulders of the mind. It escorts consciousness, and my thoughts when in the desert are on business. But my business is a strange one.

The coyote is lord of the desert, and its business in the early morning is most always food. But when it breaks off from hunting a pocket mouse to test the air for the presence of a relative or a rival, its eyes take the opportunity to enjoy the energy of the day. With its nose at work, the coyote fixes a gaze on some far point, measuring, I believe, the beauty of the sky, and in process the proof of its existence. When the nose has finished its sorting, it is

Joshua Tree National Monument, California

reassembled with eyes and body, and the coyote is on its way, focused again on food.

As I watch the coyote, stopped momentarily along the trail, I am also thinking about making a living, thinking about getting the coyote in my viewfinder, thinking about exposure, about composition, about keeping the camera steady. If the image is exceptional, I think about how much film is left on the roll, because with coyotes there is never time to reload.

Coyotes have learned a lot about us in the past couple of centuries. They have learned about poisoned bait, steel traps, guns, the stu-

por of our livestock, how to open garbage cans. They know where the boundaries of the national parks stop and start. A coyote with a territory inside the line walks with a cynical expression, cynical but smug. It moves around like a successful drug dealer on the verge of retirement. There is some-

3

thing uncoyote about its attitude, which is what you would expect from an animal that seeks sustenance from half-opened car windows and that ties up traffic whenever it comes alongside the road to mark territory.

On the outside of the official line that divides nature from the rest of the world are ordinary coyotes. These are free-lancers, contract workers without the reliable means of support enjoyed by those coyotes inside the park. You see these individuals only at great distances, most often heading in the opposite direction. From time to time, while lay-

ing quietly in a meadow photographing flowers or some other ornament of the earth, I have watched them passing by unaware. It was plain that these creatures were relaxed and happy, with not a trace of smugness. I felt the same way working in the desert with poppies, marigolds and owl's clover on every side, the atmosphere

4

Desert marigolds, Barrego Springs, California

In time of rain I come:
I can sing among the flowers:
I utter my song: my heart is
glad.

Water of flowers foams over
the earth:
My heart was intoxicated.

Aztec

5

8

*Men say they know many
things;
But lo! they have taken
wings,—
The arts and sciences,
And a thousand appliances;
The wind that blows
Is all that any body knows.*

Henry D. Thoreau

*Curve-billed thrasher, Saguaro National Monument, Arizona
Preceding pages: Globe mallow, Rattlesnake Canyon, Idaho*

laced with bird melody, red and orange rock clumped along the horizon, all of it with me stretched out in the dirt at the foot of the sky. It's a place that rests in the center of the mind.

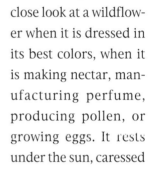

Wildflowers are what bring me to the desert. Most of them bloom in early spring when the air is cool and pleasant and when there is the entertainment of birds and animals starting new families. I don't know the desert very well at other times of the year, when temperatures are unbearably hot or cold, when weather has siphoned the color and vigor from the landscape leaving only the twisting bones of hope and memory.

My favorite deserts are the Sonoran deserts of Arizona and the Chihuahuan deserts of Texas. I visit them in April, wildflower season. Unlike coyotes, wildflowers refrain from an over display of attitude. They simply appear to enjoy themselves and that makes for pleasant companionship. You're most likely to take a close look at a wildflower when it is dressed in its best colors, when it is making nectar, manufacturing perfume, producing pollen, or growing eggs. It rests under the sun, caressed by breezes, engaged in some happy reproductive activity or some happy foreplay to reproductive activity. Wildflowers are the desert's laughter, the quiet music decorating naked mesas and flinted canyons.

Wildflowers are excuses for desert loitering. I spend time studying their form. Studying is not quite the right word; it implies a worthwhile result and there is not much to be gleaned from a close examination of the silky petals of an evening primrose or the waxy smoothness of the

9

Owl's clover and Mexican poppies, Arizona

It is above that you and I shall go;
Along the Milky Way you and I shall go;
Along the flower trail you and I shall go;
Picking flowers on our way you and I shall
go.

Wintu

claret cup's blooms. You can't eat it or sell it for publication in a calendar. Claret cups, lupines, and paintbrushes are generally distractions. They distract you from driving if they happen to be growing near the road. They distract nature lovers from productive labor. They have distracted me from steering a painless course through the desert's collection of cholla, barrel, prickly pear, saguaro, beavertail, and hedgehog cacti.

You step off the trail into the cactus forest and apprehension moves through the hairs on your back. At first you are wary of the great bristle of weaponry that aims at you from every bush, stump, clump, cushion, and pillar of dull green. You move about with arms  pressed tightly against the rib cage and limit the speed at which you turn your head toward a bird song. But by mid-morning, the dreamy atmosphere (maybe it's hunger) va-

Here is a lumbering humblebee, probing these tiny flowers. It is a rather ludicrous sight. Of course they will not support him, except a little where they are densest; so he can bend them down rapidly (hauling them in with his arms, as it were), one after another, thrusting his beak into the tube of each. It takes him but a moment to dispatch one. It is a singular sight, a humblebee clambering over a bed of these delicate flowers.

Henry D. Thoreau

12

Desert penstemon, Arizona

White-winged doves on ocotillo, Sonoran desert, Arizona

When I made you, I loved you.
Now I pity you.

I gave you all you needed:
bed of earth, blanket of blue air—

As I get further away from you
I see you more clearly.
Your souls should have been immense
by now,
not what they are,
small talking things—

Louise Glück

porizes the limits of safe space and gravity. Weightlessness displaces consciousness. You weave among the scattered monuments of saguaro, soar through draws crowded with golden brittlebush, bank past rock faces where strawberry cacti are arranged in tiers like fruit at a supermarket, dive under the arching limbs of palo verde, glide low and steady over plains of blue lupine and golden poppy. Barrel rolls scroll azure and cumulous and flashes of sun.

The sky turns a deeper shade of blue and sighting a coyote is no longer a possibility. They have retreated from the sun to coyote hiding places. Only field researchers profess to know their midday whereabouts, but the information is classified. Jackrabbits wiggle themselves into depressions under shade bushes and issue orders for the lowering of cars like taking down the flag at the end of the day outside the courthouse. They pull

15

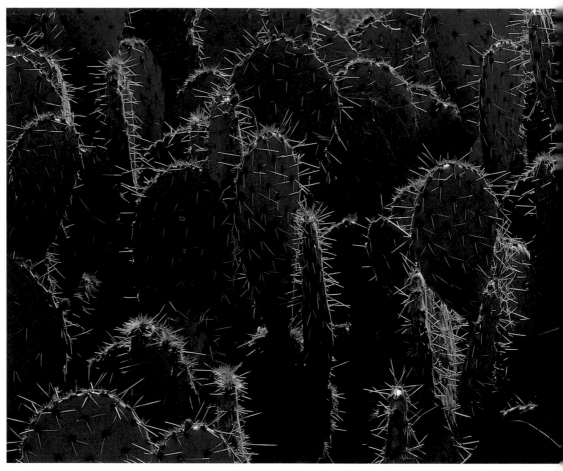

Prickly pear cactus, Anza Borrego Desert, California

tight the drawstrings around their eyes. The brain is curtained off to sleep and dream away the heat of the day.

All of this comes to you remote from automobiles, schedules, televisions, and competition.  Sensation and simplicity merge in a narcotic balm. That's when the cactus bites, like an angry, scared dog that rises up against its chain with a shaking of fur and loosing of drool, eyes shot with red and moving from side to side while the head, hanging low and steady, sends out a dark rumble of sound in the direction of its fear.

II

Glacier Lily (*Erythronium grandiflorum*) Flowers: bright yellow, pendant, one or two on a slender stalk; each 1 to 2 inches long, of six similar separate segments, recurved at the tips; 6 stamens; 3 lobed stigma. Fruit: a dry triangular, many sided capsule

Mountain Meadows
A Melody of Accelerating Amplitude

It loops through the rocks and stunted fir trees. It sails over wildflowers and frothy streams. It shoots across the rumple of green meadow. Your eyes chase the sound but it stops before they can catch up. You search among columbines and red paintbrushes for some leftover that might confirm the sound's brief claim on your attention. But your eyes are overmatched by the details of the mountain setting and luck is the only thing that brings them unexpectedly to the hummingbird. It sits on a sprig, unaware of itself, ignorant of its shimmering, voltaic magnificence, preoccupied with a few feathers in need of preening. It uses a bill half the size of a toothpick to comb and relock the tiny barbs that keep its plumage in place.

As you are watching, the hummingbird rises a foot or so from the branch. The purr of sound starts up again and the meadow

Orange sneezeweeds and red paintbrushes, San Juan Mountains, Colorado

reappears from some optical sidelot cluttered with graying dog turds and glass shards, a visual plane not available to conscious thought. In this forgotten neighborhood, anxieties are like reflections on the inner surface of a fish bowl, drawing the mind through water, nose and slobber locked onto a trail of

intoxicating scent, a scent that might lead you home to an elemental shore where winds wrap you in turquoise warmth and crystal waters serve up sweet fish seasoned by soft brown hands. It seems that the hummingbird knows these shores—and I have found this meadow.

It lies two miles above the sea in the San Juan Mountains of southern Colorado. For nine months of the year it is imprisoned by snow. In July the sun brings reprieve. *Blip, blip, blip* . . . ice becoming water. It slides off one rock and collides with another below. The music starts with this simple melody and grows with accelerating amplitude and complexity as heat transforms the mountainside from an icehouse furnished in soundless echoes to an enticement of color and clean breezes braided and draped over looming inclines

of granite and spongy soil. With the change in season, flies, bees, butterflies, birds, ground squirrels, deer, and bears arrive from stream beds and rock fissures, from lower elevations and southern latitudes, convening hungrily on the burgeoning meadow.

Where the snow has melted, the alpine meadows are sheathed in green, the surface of which is sprinkled lightly with the yellow, red, and blue of blossoms. The color draws the eye and presses flat the greenery until it becomes most of what you see. When the wind stirs, the flowers reach up with sculpted fingers to tickle the underbelly of the atmo-

*And we came to the Isle of
  Flowers: their breath met us
  out on the seas,*
*For the Spring and the middle
  Summer sat each on the lap of
  the breeze . . .*
*And the topmost spire of the
  mountain was lilies in lieu of
  snow.*
*And the lilies like glaciers winded
  down, running out below*
*Thro' the fire of the tulip and
  poppy, the blaze of gorse, and
  the blush*
*Of millions of roses that sprang
  without leaf or a thorn from the
  bush . . .*

Alfred, Lord Tennyson

23

*Wild blue flax and desert buckwheat, Grand Teton
National Park, Wyoming*

Red paintbrushes, Yankee Boy Basin, Colorado

What shall I do? My man compares me
to a wild red flower.
When I have withered in his hands,
he will leave me.

Aztec

25

sphere, the whirl of pigments tossing themselves into the whispering layers that move away, like the hummingbird, on a trail of sensation that leaves your head immersed in transparent impressions, impressions that are yet full and pleasant, that lay in the margins of physical and spiritual comfort like a dog holding warm and steady against your knee out of sight under the desk.

As the snow dissolves in the sun and seeps into the soil, the bulbs and basal leaves of the red columbine are stirred by returning energy. The columbine and the hummingbird are intimates. The columbine's petals are shaped into warm, scented tubes and the bird's bill into a probing siphon that fits the columbine nearly curve for curve. The tubes are the length of the hummingbird's bill. They contain nectar at their extremities, a reward for the bird's tolerance, for as its tongue mops up liquid, the flower splashes its face with pollen. Once the hummingbird draws its reward, it speeds off to penetrate another blossom which again bathes its tongue with sweetness as it sponges pollen from the bird's forehead. Thus the hummingbird is fed and the flowers are fertilized in a game which has no end and no discernible beginning.

While the hummingbird hovers before the columbine, its heart beats about 2500 times each minute. Thinking of this against the roughly three year lifespan of the bird provokes a cynical suspicion. When you are born, you are awarded a fixed number of heartbeats by a celestial lottery system. The amount of the award is kept secret, of course, and to be fair, everything gets about the same number of beats—roughly three billion.

Hummingbird among wild carrot, Yankee Boy Basin, Colorado
Following pages: Mule deer eating lupine, Green Mountain, Vancouver Island

You can see why the hummingbird's life passes in a flash and the elephant's and the tortoise's (45 or so beats per minute) may last over a hundred years. Like all lotteries, this one has its winners and losers, but the surprise here is for the losers. Usually you read about them in the

paper. Sometimes the news is brought to the front door after nightfall by shy men in suits.

Alpine flowers are engaged in a race with the seasons, striving to stretch out a new rhizome or drop a casting of seeds before the return of winter. The columbine, glacier lily, and geranium spread their genes about the meadow on the wings of butterfly, bee, and hummingbird, engineering the service with seductive advertising and payments of nectar. A few

Inebriate of air am I,
And debauchee of dew,
Reeling, through endless summer days,
From inns of molten blue.

When landlords turn the drunken bee
Out of the foxglove's door,
When butterflies renounce their dreams,
I shall but drink the more!

Emily Dickinson

Penstemons and scarlet trumpets near Crested Butte, Colorado

others throw their spores onto the wind, millions at a time, trusting that the fallout will somewhere give the wheel another spin, re-energizing a cycle millions of years old.

I see the cycles. I hunker among them as I am photographing. They are evident in the whirl of leaves around the stem of a mountain lily and the concentric pattern of petals on a sunflower. I  know them in the shunting of nutrients from daisy leaf to marmot to grizzly bear to bear droppings to daisy root. The cycles pulse through the intricate green systems that stand inches from my face. Hunched over, I smell the old thickness of the earth rising out of the wounds my boots have torn in the soil. Even this seems to circle, waxing and waning each time it coils over my nostrils, hinting with every pass that it will never release me.

Yet my thoughts continue to run out in straight lines, following pathways printed on spreadsheets, obeying directives written in legislatures, searching out progress and measuring it against time.

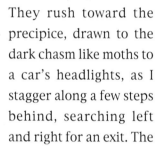 They rush toward the precipice, drawn to the dark chasm like moths to a car's headlights, as I stagger along a few steps behind, searching left and right for an exit. The meadow offers exits familiar to me but these sidepaths are not well marked and I cannot follow them for long.

Now I find another—a black bear whose weak eyes have failed to identify me, its ancient enemy squatting motionless under the Indian hellebore, armed not with spear or rock but cameras. It

The West of which I speak is but
another name for the Wild; and what
I have been preparing to say is, that
in Wildness is the preservation of the
World . . . . It was because the
children of the Empire were not
suckled by the wolf that they were
conquered and displaced by the
children of the northern forest who
were. I believe in the forest, and in
the meadow, and in the night in
which the corn grows.

34

Henry D. Thoreau

Sticky geranium, Yellowstone National Park, Wyoming
Preceding page: Blue columbine, Colorado

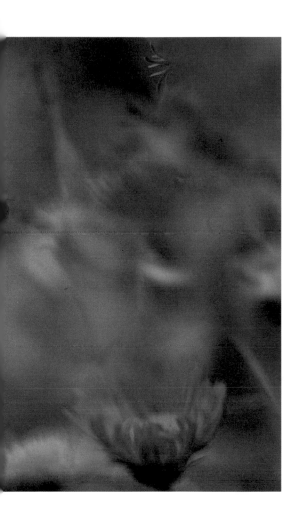

wanders closer and I see its breath stirring little puffs of dust under the muzzle. I can see the supple lips pulling up

plants. The nose is working, opening and closing, sampling the meadow, guiding the lips and tongue on a journey of ingestion, a journey as significant as Magellan's or Armstrong's depending how far you wish to step back to take your measurement. And for a while I am a long way out looking back; I have joined the bear and the hummingbird.

III

Wild Gaillardia (*Gaillardia aristata*) Flowers: ray-florets yellow streaked with purple, 10 to 18 with wedge-shaped 3 cleft rays; disk-florets purplish-brown, numerous with both stamens and pistil; involucral bracts hairy; flower heads large, showy, sol-

Prairie Meadows
Recollections of Spent Romance

There is no light, nor air, nor a chance of a drink of rain for the grama and little bluestem grasses, for the gaillardias and asters that lie under the fallen buffalo. Likely injured on the highway, it has staggered a few hundred yards, collapsed, and died in the meadow. Like most dead things with back bones, it projects magnetism of a kind that is usually unwelcome, like a second helping of gravy if you happen to be on a diet.

But I am enjoying this viewing. It's sunny and warm; for the time being the air smells fresh and I can barely hear the vehicles that pass by occasionally behind the swell of land that screens me from the road. In front of me on the Wyoming prairie rests this great lump of upholstered meat. The sun has only been up a short time and I can clearly hear the meadowlarks yodelling for a half

Meadowlark near Cheyenne, Oklahoma

mile in every direction. Like other prairie birds, their voices are powerful to penetrate the winds that sweep across the land unimpeded by forest or hill. Beyond the buffalo, a jackrabbit watches me through the grasses

and forbs. Most of the plants are native but many are species introduced by European settlers.

I am sitting on the ground, legs stretched out with the rest of me propped up on a locked arm. I'm too accustomed to chairs to find it comfortable to sit cross-legged like the Indians that once lived in these meadows. In those days life on the prairie was like sailing on a sea of grass. The land knew early fame among Europeans for its oceanic emptiness, a sweep of undulating tan and green, a repose of wild turf receding distantly into vapors fused with the sky. The prairie was by and large flat, like the sea, but it tilted this way and that like swells coming under a bow. Everything the Indians needed  was on board, that is, inside the tipi—things to cook with, things to sleep with, probably some leftovers from supper the night before, a few medicines. Approaching winter, there would be extra provisions to bring them through that portion of the voyage. They had to haul this along when they quartered up or down the prairie a ways, but there wasn't much to it and generally they were free to roam.

Nobody owned much of anything because there was no advantage. The Indians had food, they had shelter, and they took entertainment from each other and the tasks of daily life. The land seemed limitless, so there was no need to draw serious boundaries. They didn't need vacations because, in their mind, they never went to work. Life passed with hunting, fishing, collecting berries, setting snares,

vening primrose and sleepy daisy meadow near Giddings, Texas

Drifting meadow of air,
Where bloom the daisied banks
and violets,
And in whose fenny labyrinth
The bittern booms and heron
wades;
Spirit of lakes and seas and rivers,
Bear only perfumes and the scent
Of healing herbs to just men's
fields!

Henry D. Thoreau

Indian blankets, Texas

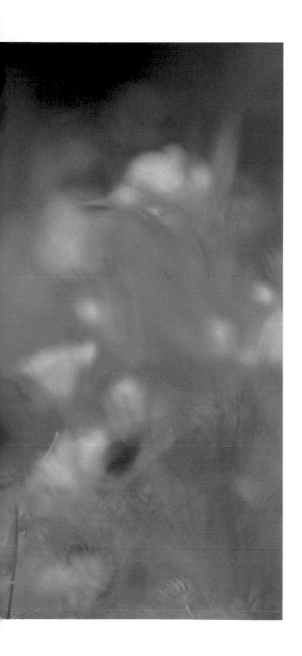

Butterfly, butterfly, butterfly, butterfly,
Oh, look, see it hovering among the flowers,
It is like a baby trying to walk and not knowing
how to go.
The clouds sprinkle down the rain.

Acoma

44

Grasses, Oklahoma
Pages 46-47: Pointed phlox, Texas

and sometimes running a small garden. A buffalo hunt was the greatest of pleasures. The buffalo was the basis of the Indian's existence, and the buffalo's existence was grass.

There is a lot of grass standing up around my buffalo, which by the way, still hasn't moved. Among the grasses are forbs, the name given to leafy plants by botanists. Forbs are what most people think of as wildflowers. Buffaloes ordinarliy don't eat them for some reason, but pronghorn antelopes do. Consequently pronghorns and buffaloes get along together and in the old days you would see them feeding side-by-side, one with head low, the other with head a little higher, but both heads down chomping. Their eyes were perched high on the skull where they could keep a lookout for predators—the grizzlies, wolves, and cougars that commonly stalked among the wild roses and cinquefoils a couple of centuries ago.

From my reclined perspective, little of the change of the past two hundred years is evident. No wires, poles, fences, highways, malls, or feedlots to contaminate the currents of my reverie. (Even now a buffalo lies beside me.) Forbs are bursting into flower everywhere. Should I lie flat on the prairie . . . the sky spreads out behind the slender extensions of wheatgrass and the yellow-orange of a gaillardia that leans into my line of vision. My ears are flooded with subtle energies—the footsteps of foxes and the slide of garter snakes, the scratching and sniffing of mice and gophers, the chew of beetles and prairie

45

dogs, the flutter of butterflies, bobolinks, and larks, the hum of bees, the swoop of flies, the clatter of grasshoppers, the excavations of a distant badger, the shuffling of grasses and wildflowers by gentle winds—all blended in a balm of sounds circulating in the clear pool of a generous sky. It ebbs and flows, breaking over my ears.

My body floats on a mattress of stems, roots, and air. The buffalo and I are on the same tack, noses pointed at the West, bellies stuffed with snips and grindings of fresh greens, feeling warm and sleepy, brains locked together in a bloodshot recollection of spent romance.

From inside this delirium, my vision picks up a movement, a twitching on the buffalo's hairy topography as a long muscle contracts somewhere in its interior. Then I notice the hooves kicking in circular spasms, like the split, dirt-caked pads of an old dog dreaming on the kitchen linoleum. The dark mound begins to rock and suddenly the buffalo is on its feet. It doesn't move at first, as if trying to regain its balance on a pitching deck. Grasses lean against the dark fetlocks that now stand like pilings inches from my eyes. I look past them onto the patch of herbs where the animal had lain. It is pressed into a single, anemic dimension, looking like a page from a school girl's botany text, layered with loose samples picked on an outing. These specimens are broken and twisted as you would expect, and slimy where the weight of the buffalo has burst open the cells and freed the juice inside.

A bee appears, circles the closest leg and lands on the gaillardia where it begins to graze among the stamens and pistils,

Winecups and Texas ragwort, Texas

Gaillardia near Carlsbad, New Mexico

To make a prairie it takes a
clover and one bee.—
One clover, and a bee,
And revery.
The revery alone will do
If bees are few.

Emily Dickinson

vacuuming up bits of pollen with its proboscis. The buffalo moves off over the swell of prairie. A stream of sunlight is caught in the dust which rises from its footsteps. The light lingers in the margins of the beast's coat which hangs nearly to the ground in places, clotted with mud and shit. The buffalo walks over the ridge into a golden luminence—Heaven, I think, or at least, paradise. But then the fly is on my face. My eyes open and the buffalo still rests silently on the prairie beside me, an island sinking in a bottomless sea.

51

IV

Orange Hawkweed (*Hieracium aurantiacum*) Flowers: ray-florets red-orange with both stamens and pistil; disk-florets none; involucre bracts with dark glandular hairs; flower heads—1 inch across, several in compact cluster. Fruit: a dry achene

Wayside Meadows
Surrendering to Primitive Instincts

With every step I jostle a few plants, shaking out a sprinkle of dew onto my boots. My pants are already soaked from the knees down. Despite the wetness, the walking is easy because the vegetation is thin and composed of only a few species arranged in patches. Hawkweeds and ox-eye daisies dominate this hastily assembled community growing in an upland meadow of the Finger Lakes district of New York. In this region, the variety of wildflowers is cosmopolitan with species from all over the planet cropping up in areas where the native forest has been removed—roadsides, pastures, power corridors—any place a bulldozer, backhoe, or plough has set its teeth.

Immigrants are plentiful because they need not adapt to the ecological constraints of established plant communities. In the race for sunlight, moisture, and soil nutrients, every species starts

54

Hawkweed meadow, New Brunswick

from the same line of exposed, naked earth. Those from Europe have trained for centuries for such races, sprinting alongside the cobblestone roadways and aqueducts radiating from Rome, Aix-en-Provence, or Bath.

They have followed the ox and the plough through the fields of Tuscany and Ukraine, thrusting out rhizomes and stolons, hurling their seeds like javelins at any patch of bare earth, range and marksmanship improving with each successive generation.

55

European settlers brought thousands of varieties of seeds to North America. Some were thrown mistakenly into bags of seeds intended to establish a continental agriculture in the American wilderness. Others made the Atlantic crossing in the pockets and pant cuffs of farm boys. Still others were ingredients of herbal teas, medicines, dyes, and perfumes. By accident or intent they were loosed on the American soil. They raced like Miami gray hounds through ploughed fields and gouged hillsides while homegrown species were still hunting up a familiar shade tree where they could flop down and chew at fleas. Unfortunately, the trees had been toppled, sawed, and stacked for lumber and fuel. A lot of the forest was burnt down summarily to make room for roadways, facto-ries, and wheat fields. By the time the scent of this strange activity wafted past the noses of the complacent natives, the newcomers had already lifted a leg and claimed the territory for king and czar.

Hawkweed did well on the American frontier. It blooms with the warm, eerie radiance of the sun setting behind a Los Angeles smog, a hue irresistible to insects. Sometimes two honey bees feed side by side on the same flower head, rooting into the bundles of pistils

56

Simple and fresh and fair from winter's close emerging, As if no artifice of fashion, business, politics has ever been, Forth from its sunny nook of shelter's grass-innocent, golden, calm as dawn,

Walt Whitman

Mustard field, Waterloo County, Ontario
Following pages: Blue flags near Ithaca, New York

60

Cattail and purple loosestrife near Perth, Ontario

The bee is not afraid of me,
I know the butterfly;
The pretty people in the
woods
Receive me cordially.
The brooks laugh louder
when I come,
The breezes madder play.
Wherefore, mine eyes, thy
silver mist?
Wherefore, O summer's day?

Emily Dickinson

and stamens, bumping into each other as they concentrate on their work. Bees hover and streak about the blossoms, changing course without warning. Time is short and their industry is determined. As I move through the plants, the bees emerge from tufted petals, making a quick lopsided circle or two before they head off, irritated at the disturbance al-

though not enough to think about doing me harm. They sting judiciously for they can only do it once and this is followed soon after by death. If you have been stung, the degree of your transgression in the mind of the honey bee (now certainly dead) was without equal.

I am several times guilty of transgression. When I was five years old, I caught honey bees that visited the dandelions growing in the ditch in front of the house. I scooped them off the blossoms in a big pickle jar which later served as their resettlement chamber. The jar had a punched lid for fresh air and an interior furnished with a few blades of grass for the bees to sleep on, or take exercise with, or eat, or weave into a hive so they wouldn't get homesick. The utility of the grass was never clearly established in my mind. In retrospect, I realize it was thin payment, provoked by subconscious guilt, for the pleasure I derived from their incarceration. One day, in a swell of friendship, I wrapped my hands around a bee gorging in the center of a dandelion. My belief in the spirit of love was high, my touch was gentle and my motives benign, but in a second or two I experienced a stab of pain from the general vicinity of the bee. My hands flew open. I headed for mother at top speed, having received a lesson in love that would not take hold

62

Dame's rocket and hemlock parsley, New Yo

I know a bank where the wild thyme blows,
Where oxlips and nodding violet grows,
Quite over-canopied with luscious woodbine,
With sweet musk-roses, and with eglantine.

William Shakespeare

63

for several decades. In the interim, my life entered the world of bees and near bees in

earnest, and I came to capture them (on film) for my livelihood as well as my pleasure.

My latest transgression took place, oddly, in a bag of Doritos while I was birdwatching from the front seat of my truck. A finger provoked the ultimate sacrifice as it was engaged in a pincer movement with a thumb. The intent of the maneuver is obvious, but I snagged a honey bee instead of a corn chip. It sank its stinger into my finger tip, injecting a flush of poison into the nerve-packed epidermis. Strangely, the pain thrilled me. It was focused on a tiny locale of no strategic value except for reading a menu or playing checkers, neither of which was contemplated. Nevertheless, the sensation was overpowering. I groaned and giggled over the pain and the insignificance of its consequence.

64

More than you love me, very possibly
you love the beasts of the field, even,
possibly, the field itself, in August dotted
with wild chicory and aster:
I know. I have compared myself
to those flowers, their range of feeling
so much smaller and without issue . . . .

Louise Glück

Downy woodpecker feeding on mullein near
Richmond, Indiana

Cattails and wild roses, Montana

As a young man, I used to walk with my dog in the meadows near my various, successive homes in the eastern part of the continent. He was a Chihuahua named Carlos, not exactly a field dog, but his bow legs were no stranger to high grass. He had a sense of humor.

His small size meant that he was entertained by things that wouldn't phase a Labrador or Rottweiler. Butterflies were his particular delight. 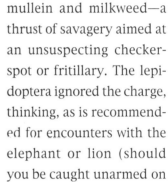 Designed to pose in a coffee cup rather than point up a covey of quail, Carlos would take off after a butterfly at first sight without consideration of strategy or the nature of the impending conflict. He bolted, a flash of muscle and ferocity moving beneath the fabric of the meadow. The line of his attack was visible as a thin seam of trembling vegetation as he brushed past the daisies and campions, shaking vetches and chicories, powering his way over clumps of celandine and buttercup, skirting the thick stems of mullein and milkweed—a thrust of savagery aimed at an unsuspecting checkerspot or fritillary. The lepidoptera ignored the charge, thinking, as is recommended for encounters with the elephant or lion (should you be caught unarmed on the open savannah) that it is best to out "bluff" the assailant. But Carlos didn't know the meaning of the word and he pressed the attack home dependably whenever possible. At the critical moment, he leaped clear of the meadow like a Polaris missile erupting from a north Atlantic swell, lips retracted over snapping teeth. They invariably came up

67

Sow thistle and vetches near Langhorn, Pennsylvania

empty. After surrendering to this primitive instinct a few times, Carlos would lie down in

the meadow to recover, once again the philosopher.

I take a seat among the hawkweeds, leaning back on a cushion of grasses and herbs, remembering the days when I used to nap alongside Carlos, sometimes watching the meadow and the sky reflected in his brown eyes which never stopped moving as long as there was a butterfly on the wing.

The photographs in this book were made with Canon 35 mm single-lens-reflex cameras and special close-up focusing devices needed to attain magnified views of the flowers. Fujichrome Velvia transparency film was used except for a few images which were made on Kodachrome 64.

When photographing wildflowers, it is customary to use a standard or short tele-photo lens (50 to 100 mm) in conjunction with extension tubes or bellows which allow for closer-than-normal focusing. However, for many of these pictures, I used a 500 mm super-telephoto lens which produces photographs with a limited range of sharp focus. I wasn't as interested in what was to be rendered sharply as I was in

what would appear as washes of blurred color. My standard technique was to set up the heavy camera, lens, and bellows apparatus on a tripod at the same level as the flowers. Then by panning the lens back and forth and focusing in and out, I would sift through the meadow for a com-position. Due to the extreme focal length of the lens, a blossom even slightly out-of-focus lost all detail and appeared as a pool of color. Normally I tried to anchor the design to one or two blossoms that were rendered sharply. It can take an hour to get set up and sort out a suitable image, longer if you choose to wait for a bee or butterfly to en-liven the scene. It's an enjoyable way to spend time and catch up on your dreaming.

Indian blankets, Texas

Sources

Desert Meadows

Page 5 Angel Garibay. "Song of Birds", *La Literatura de los Aztecas.* ©1964, p. 84-85. (In time of rain I come . . .)

Page 8 Henry D. Thoreau. *Collected Poems of Henry D. Thoreau.* Edited by Carl Bode, Baltimore: John Hopkins University Press, ©1970, p. 135. (Men say they know many things; . . .)

Page 11 D. Demetracopoulou. "You and I Shall Go", *Anthropos*, vol. 30. ©1935, p. 485. (It is above that you and I shall go . . .)

Page 12 Henry D. Thoreau. *The Journal of Henry D. Thoreau, vol. XII* Edited by Bradford Torrey and Francis H. Allen, ed., Boston: Houghton & Mifflin Co., ©1906, p. 278. (Here is a lumbering bumblebee . . .)

Page 15 Louise Glück. "Vespers", *The Wild Iris* by Louise Glück. Hopewell,: The Ecco Press, ©1993, p. 15. Reprinted by permission of the publisher. (When I made you, I loved you . . .)

Mountain Meadows

Page 25 Miguel León-Portilla. "The Woman's Complaint", *Pre-Columbian Literatures of Mexico.* Norman, OK: University Press of Oklahoma. ©1969, p. 114-115. (What shall I do? My man compares me to a wild red flower . . .)

Page 30 Emily Dickinson. *Selected Poems & Letters of Emily Dickinson.* Edited by Thomas H. Johnson. Cambridge, Mass.: The Belknap Press of Harvard University Press. ©1951, 1955,

1979, 1983, p. 71-72. Reprinted by permission of the publisher. (Inebriate of air am I . . .)

Page 34 Thoreau. "The Wild", *Thoreau's Vision: The Major Essay*. Englewood Cliffs, NJ: Prentice-Hall, Inc. ©1973, p. 144. (The West of which I speak . . .)

Prairie Meadows

Page 41 Thoreau. "Mist", *Walden and Civil Disobedience*. New York: NAL Penguin Inc. ©1960, p. 245. (Drifting meadow of air . . .)

Page 43 Frances Densmore. " Butterfly Song", *Music of Acoma, Isleta, Cochiti and Zuni Pueblos*. Washington, D.C.: Bureau of American Ethnology, Bulletin 165. ©1957, p. 38. (Butterfly, butterfly, butterfly . . .)

Page 51 Dickinson. *Selected Poems*. ©1983, p. 204. Reprinted by permission of the publisher. (To make a prairie it takes a clover and one bee . . .)

Pacific Coast

Page 60 Dickinson. *Selected Poems*. ©1983, p. 49. Reprinted by permission of the publisher. (The bee is not afraid of me . . .)

Page 65 Glück. "Vespers" *The Wild Iris*. ©1993, p. 38. Reprinted by permission of the publisher. (More than you love me . . .)

PRODUCED BY TERRAPIN BOOKS
Santa Fe, New Mexico